Participatory Budgeting
and Civic Tech

Related Digital Shorts from Georgetown University Press

Crowdsourcing in the Public Sector
by Daren C. Brabham

The Ethical Lobbyist: Reforming Washington's Influence Industry
by Thomas T. Holyoke

Talking Politics? What You Need to Know before Opening Your Mouth
by Sheila Suess Kennedy

Participatory Budgeting and Civic Tech

The Revival of Citizen Engagement

Hollie Russon Gilman

GEORGETOWN UNIVERSITY PRESS

Library of Congress Cataloging-in-Publication Data

Names: Gilman, Hollie Russon, author.
Title: Participatory budgeting and civic tech : the revival of citizen
    engagement / Hollie Russon Gilman.
Description: Washington, DC : Georgetown University Press, 2016. | Includes
    bibliographical references.
Identifiers: LCCN 2016007093 (print) | LCCN 2016008596 (ebook) | ISBN
    9781626163409 (pb : alk. paper) | ISBN 9781626163416 (eb)
Subjects: LCSH: Local budgets—United States—Citizen participation. | Local
    finance—United States.
Classification: LCC HJ9147 .G55 2016 (print) | LCC HJ9147 (ebook) | DDC
    352.4/82140973—dc23
LC record available at http://lccn.loc.gov/2016007093

♾This book is printed on acid-free paper meeting the requirements of the American National Standard for Permanence in Paper for Printed Library Materials.

17 16   9 8 7 6 5 4 3 2 First printing

Printed in the United States of America

Contents

Preface

ONE EVENING OVER DINNER while I was a doctoral student I was intro-
duced to Joe Moore, a Chicago alderman—the first elected official to implement participatory budgeting (PB) in the United States. Through PB, the
alderman put discretionary "Menu Money," about $1.3 million, into the
hands of the ward's residents. PB is a democratic process to empower citizens to decide on public budget allocations and vote on where and how to
implement. Unlike other processes, PB creates a mechanism for binding
citizen input in decision making.

Chicago—of all places—seemed an unlikely candidate for democratic
innovation in the United States. However, as I listened, I found myself
listening to an inspiring story about community members working
together, meeting new people, and working in tandem with elected officials. Most of all, people received an interactive and creative form of civic
education. This was not a traditional class in civics but rather an opportunity for a hands-on experience in finding out how precisely to turn ideas
into policy.

Several years after this dinner conversation, I joined the Obama administration to help execute the second-term open government agenda. Part
of my goal in working in the Office of Science and Technology Policy was
to think about the opportunities and challenges of leveraging technology
and including PB within broader United States commitments under the
Open Government Partnership. In 2011 President Barack Obama launched

the Open Government Partnership along with Brazil, Indonesia, Mexico, Norway, the Philippines, South Africa, and the United Kingdom. To date, it includes sixty-six nations. Countries in this multilateral partnership commit to greater citizen participation, collaboration, and transparency in governance. Each member country is required to submit a national action plan outlining its domestic open government commitments.

Part of the appeal of PB is precisely its transnational path to prominence. The process began in Porto Alegre, Brazil, in 1989 after a twenty-year military dictatorship and first came to the United States in 2009. PB is a transnational innovation, leveraging insight from the Global South to the United States. Understanding its current manifestations in the United States helps shed light on the growing trend of civic innovation happening in the United States and globally. I argue that PB is one promising democratic experiment within a larger tool kit to reimagine the relationship between citizens and their governance institutions. PB can add to and enhance the existing civic infrastructure and further democratic experimentation. This publication is motivated by the desire to examine the intersection of civic engagement with institutions of governance within the larger movement to capitalize on new technology to improve democracy. This family of innovations has potential to usher in a new type of public sphere where everyday people have more interaction and engagement with their institutions.

This public sphere will involve networked community and in-person deliberation and dialogue. Technology is a necessary part of the equation. I view democracy as an opportunity for self-renewal and human expression in a public sphere. As social reformer John Dewey notes, "Life is a self-renewing process through action upon the environment."[1] If democracy is ultimately the sum of its people, each generation faces an opportunity to reimagine the democratic experience. Digital tools can help support the opportunities to reduce barriers to entry, bring new information into the public sphere, and increase the opportunities for people to monitor their government.

However, the precise pathways through which democratic deepening takes place and the use of digital tools require further research. In order to shed light on the emerging phenomena, I combine empirical results with a theoretical and normative framework. I employ a variety of methods, including formal interviews, field observations, site visits, process tracing, difference-in-difference analysis, and electronic sources. I have tried to be clear where my claims rest on personal observations based on my extensive firsthand experience of PB.

Much further research is needed in this emerging space to understand what works and why. This work is but one attempt to begin the conversation, outlining why inclusive governance and innovations are important in the face of rising declines in institutional trust. It provides an introduction to inclusive governance and articulates a framework for understanding civic innovation in the United States. It then provides an in-depth examination of PB and its implementation in New York City. The goal is to illustrate how a given innovation takes root in a highly context-specific environment. I end by providing further examples of civic innovation and policy recommendations geared toward both researchers and practitioners.

This work is influenced by research conducted over several years. For an extended take on these topics, see my full-length book *Democracy Reinvented* (2016), published in the Harvard Kennedy School's Innovative Governance in the 21st Century series with Brookings Institution Press.[2] I conducted case study research on three pilots of PB in the United States (Chicago, New York City, and Boston), analyzing each in order to synthesize common recommendations informed by experience working closely with practitioners and as a policymaker.

The work of building the body of quantitative and qualitative research that will support PB and other civic innovations in the United States is just getting started. Rather than offering a complete history of PB or a comprehensive study of any one instance of PB, my goal is to provide a rich and multifaceted analysis of an emerging civic process while also generating a theoretical understanding applicable beyond PB. In New York City, the Community Development Project at the Urban Justice Center led the research and evaluation of the process and worked to organize graduate students, professors, and practitioners in the field of PB to draft surveys to be administered at different phases of the process—during the neighborhood assemblies, budget delegate committees, and at the vote.[3]

Participatory Budgeting and Civic Tech

Introduction

AROUND THE WORLD, citizens are deeply disaffected with the basic institutions and leaders they elect to govern them.[1] Looking at almost any indicator of satisfaction reveals the troubling news. The United States is no exception. To take one recent example, a poll run by Gallup in 2014 found that only 30 percent of Americans say they have "a great deal" or "quite a lot" of confidence in the Supreme Court; 29 percent, in the presidency; and 7 percent, in the U.S. Congress. Evidently, the perception that Washington is broken is a view shared by all generations. The millennial generation—those born between the early 1980s and the early 2000s—shows decreased participation in the traditional forms of civic engagement beyond voting, such as joining groups and unions, contacting public officials, attending public meetings, and working with neighbors.[2] But trust in and satisfaction with governing institutions is integral for a functioning democracy, and believing that the system works is a core underpinning of representative democracy.

Partly in response to this growing disaffection, a wave of participatory policy reform has emerged in America's largest cities, capitalizing on new technology to improve democracy. This movement—collectively known as open government, civic innovation, civic tech, participatory democracy, or inclusive governance—is engaging policymakers, citizens, and civil society and is reinvigorating democratic instincts that have long lain dormant.

Civic tech on its own is a term lacking a standardized definition because some for-profit entities are sometimes included in the analysis.[3] *I define civic tech as leveraging digital tools to improve democratic governance toward more transparency, inclusion, and participatory outcomes.* My definition of civic tech helps situate the discussion within a larger frame of participatory democracy instead of focusing merely on new Internet or smart phone applications, or "apps." I offer a definition of civic tech featuring core principles relevant for public policy. First, citizens increasingly expect more direct contact with government and expect these interactions to be technology based and as "smart" and accommodating as consumer services. Second, digital tools can empower citizens to become more active and engaged participants in their communities and contribute to government decision making.[4] Finally, technology can facilitate more direct two-way communication and government responsiveness between citizens and their government. In the public policy ideal of civic tech, government can leverage digital tools to be *smarter* (more targeted and efficient), *responsive* (to empower and communicate with citizens), and *goal oriented* toward results.[5]

Inclusive Governance

In order to work toward this model of participatory and inclusive democratic governance, I propose a multiprong strategy that recognizes both the power of traditional government as well as broader definitions of *governance* that encompasses a range of civic actors. This includes thinking beyond only *efficiency* (e.g., service delivery) toward *effectiveness* (e.g., more accountable, transparent, inclusive, participatory, representative, and responsive governance). More-inclusive governance can lead to more resilient, adaptive, and better public systems. Building "civic muscles" requires multiple entry points for citizens of diverse background to participate in a variety of ways.

Inclusive governance ought to both build the structures for citizens to have meaningful participation in governance as well as strengthen citizens' ability to participate in such structures. Governments can (and should) empower, legitimate, and structure channels for engagement working together with other sectors. Thus, inclusive governance must address the places in which government can effectively open up spaces for citizens (e.g., participatory budgeting) as well as the opportunities for citizens to self-organize to improve governance outcomes (e.g., community maker studios).

Political theorist Mark Warren has an enthusiastic list of civic virtues associated with democracy, including but not limited to attentiveness to the common good and concerns for justice; tolerance of the views of others; trustworthiness; willingness to participate, deliberate, and listen; respect for the rule of law; and respect for the rights of others.[6] These qualities matter for building more resilient systems and the civic skills necessary to participate, shape, and form these systems.

Why Participatory Budgeting?

PB is one of the most promising of these new civic innovations, in part because elected officials across the country have shown willingness to implement and sustain the process. In some places, such as New York City, PB is moving out of the realm of an ad hoc experiment and becoming integrated into how portions of municipal budgets are decided. The next section presents an in-depth examination of PB, including its largest experiment to date in New York City. The goal is to understand the context in which PB arises and how it relates to the broader trend to empower citizens as decision makers within a local context. This in turn can inform research and policy implementation of civic innovations within a variety of settings.

A news story in the *New York Times* described PB as "revolutionary civics in action."[7] PB empowers citizens to identify community needs, work with elected officials to craft budget proposals, and vote on where and how to spend public funds. Unlike other forms of civic engagement, PB involves spending real public money. Making democracy work is not just about making better citizens or changing policies. It is about creating structures and conditions that make the effective exercise of democratic citizenship possible. PB is a unique structure that does that.

PB emerged in Brazil in 1989. It arrived in the United States in 2009, when one ward in Chicago decided to try it out with a limited dedicated budget of one million dollars. Now cities across the United States are experimenting with the practice, with New York City alone putting roughly $32 million toward the 2014–2015 process.[8] In 2015 twenty-four of fifty-one New York City Council districts, representing nearly 4.5 million residents, are participating in PB. The nonprofit Participatory Budgeting Project, working with community partners, has helped seed and sustain PB's growth from Brazil to the United States.[9]

Mayors Rahm Emanuel of Chicago and Bill de Blasio of New York have pledged to greatly expand it. Cities from Boston and Cambridge, in Massachusetts, to Long Beach, San Francisco, and Vallejo, in California, are adopting PB.[10] Across the United States, cities are actively seeking adoption while adding new components, such as a youth-driven process in Boston and now Seattle.[11] Several cities are experimenting with online components, including short-message-service voting and digital voting.

As discussed later in more depth, at the end of 2013 the White House issued a pledge to support the growth of PB using existing federal community funds as part of its international effort to support open government initiatives.[12] Buffalo, New York, and other cities are already exploring how to use community development block grants from the U.S. Department of Housing and Urban Development to fund PB programs.[13]

PB has the potential to revitalize local democracy in America in a way that can be expanded across localities. I argue that PB provides a promising model for reengaging citizens in public decision making and increases trust in government. PB serves as an edifying lens through which to study participatory democracy and civic innovation because it is one of the most pervasive democratic innovations in recent decades. PB involves directly empowering ordinary citizens to generate project ideas, which they then vote into enactment. People work directly with government agencies to craft these viable budget proposals, learning about the process of governance and bureaucracy along the way. PB differs from other participatory democratic models in that elected officials pledge to implement projects voted upon by citizens. Citizens are not merely advising or consulting on decision making but instead actively craft budget policy through binding input. Citizens are involved in every critical juncture of the process, from designing their projects to voting upon which projects to enact.

PB also tends to engage citizens in hyper local projects, which provides scholars and policymakers the opportunity to understand not only what a given community needs but precisely where and how to deliver it. This takes advantage of citizen experience—people who spend their daily lives in a given location can identify the exact location for a needed new park bench, for example. Participants leave the process having transformed their relationships with their neighbors, elected officials, and community. This includes the strengthening of civil society. PB may not be a panacea for all current democratic deficits, but it is an instructive paradigm for reengaging citizens in their democracy.

Part of PB's strength as a democratic innovation lies in its focus on the level of empowering citizens as experts within the communities they know. Other democratic innovations aiming for greater participation face the challenges of integrating ideals that emerged in the small scale of the ancient polis in antiquity with the practices of contemporary democracy in the United States. Athens, the largest city-state in ancient Greece, had the quorum for assembly fixed for some purposes at 6,000 with 18,000 seats in the Pnyx where the ecclesia (assembly) met with an estimate of 40,000 adult male citizens. For Plato, 5,040 was the maximum number of people for a unit of government.[14] The polis, with its strengths and weaknesses, was inescapably local. On the local level, everyday citizens can be experts on what is the necessary funding for their community.

What Is Participatory Budgeting?

PB has expanded to over 1,500 municipalities worldwide since its inception in Porto Alegre, Brazil, in 1989 by the leftist Partido dos Trabalhadores (PT), or Worker's Party. PB expanded from Latin America to Europe beginning in 2001, with Italy, France, and Spain becoming the core countries to initially adopt it.[15] In 2014 Paris implemented the largest version of PB in Europe. It has set aside €426 million to be decided upon by residents between 2014 and 2020; the allocation in 2014–15 was roughly €20 million.[16] The World Bank and United Nations have dubbed PB a "best practice" in democratic innovation and have spent millions of dollars in aid to institute PB in places as diverse as the Democratic Republic of the Congo and the Dominican Republic.[17] Through this process, clientelism and corruption are reduced while service delivery and citizen engagement are improved.[18] PB helps foster a more transparent environment. In contrast to a closed model where elected officials make budgetary decisions, sometimes involving patronage, PB empowers citizens to generate viable budget proposals and vote on projects. Citizens can hold their elected officials to account and participate in a more open and transparent budgeting process.

Setting the starting point for PB as its use in Porto Alegre establishes a twenty-five-year history of the practice and raises the question of impact assessment. Some potential indicators of success include (1) greater citizen education, (2) more redistribution to lower-income citizens, (3) greater transparency and accountability in the budget process, and (4) a deepening of citizen engagement and furthering of democratic opportunities for citizens.[19]

Gauging the success of PB is intricately related to the criteria used for evaluation. For example, Brian Wampler's set of criteria involves "engaged deliberation, social justice, and active citizens."[20] He understands PB's success through this lens, looking at various indicators including citizen efficacy and mobilization of low-income residents.[21] Wampler's surveys assess the degree to which citizens are efficacious via the process—including in influencing and improving service delivery.[22] His depiction of successful PB requires strong networks of CSOs (civil society organizations) that exert political pressure to implement the process and move it forward. He suggests that social movements in Brazil viewed participatory mechanisms as useful tools for organization.[23]

In Brazil, PB has been shown to improve governance, reinforce democracy, and contribute significantly to the well-being of the poorest citizens.[24] Michael Touchton and Wampler connect the presence of PB in a given locality with increased municipal spending on sanitation and health, increased numbers of CSOs, and decreases in infant mortality.[25] Similarly, Sónia Gonçalves found that Brazilian municipalities that implemented PB channeled a larger fraction of their total budget to investments in sanitation and health services, with a pronounced reduction in infant mortality.[26]

At times it can be difficult to understand the precise causal mechanisms that drive these results. One challenge to isolating causal effects is variance in local city conditions. Paolo Spada argues that a clear impact of PB on public spending cannot be currently identified. The initial introduction of PB only has a demonstrable effect on the probability of reelection for the party of the mayor implementing PB.[27]

In its original campaign for PB, the PT outlined four basic guiding principles: (1) direct citizen participation in government decision-making processes and oversight; (2) administrative and fiscal transparency as a deterrent for corruption; (3) improvements in urban infrastructure and services, especially in aiding the indigent; and (4) altering political culture so that citizens can serve as democratic agents.[28]

As Brazil emerged out of nineteen years of military dictatorship, PB offered it a way to reimagine the state: "Participatory budgeting . . . would help re-legitimate the state by showing that [it] could be effective, redistributive, and transparent."[29] PB gives citizens the opportunity to learn about government practices and come together to discuss, deliberate, and, ultimately, make a substantive impact on budget allocations.[30] PB programs are implemented at the behest of citizens, governments, nongovernmental organizations (NGO), and CSOs, in order to give citizens a direct voice in budget allocations.[31] Scholars have suggested that when people engage in participatory deliberation, they are better equipped to assess the performance of elected officials on both the local and national levels.[32]

PB and related models of participatory democracy can be implemented in many different ways and adjusted to the given unique political context where it is employed. Throughout the developing world it has served as a model for citizen engagement, with successful runs in political structures as diverse as Bangladesh and South Africa. In the period after the Cold War, some newly formed democracies added participatory mechanisms into these countries' constitutional orders. For example, Bulgaria, which is a signatory to the European Charter of Local Self-Government, also created robust mechanisms for direct citizen engagement in decision making, including community meetings, regulated contact with mayors, and referendums.[33]

Three broad trends in these newly formed democracies lend themselves to PB: increased forms of participation for legitimacy, a trend toward transparency, and a trend toward fiscal decentralization.[34] PB serves as a way to legitimate and implement these ideals in practice. International organizations often partner with local NGOs on the ground to implement a variety of PB mechanisms. The forms of implementation, levels of mobilization, and degrees to which the process is binding differ across geopolitical contexts.

In newly formed democracies, PB aims to institute mechanisms of transparency and bottom-up democracy in countries that have a history of corruption.[35] The aim is more effective service delivery and greater responsiveness to local citizen needs.[36] Citizen participation improves vertical or social accountability by altering the incentive structure for officeholders. Through deepening citizen engagement, public officials have a new sense of eyes watching them and of public accountability.

How can PB fit with the context of the United States? Forms of participatory democracy already exist in the United States, including such mechanisms for citizen feedback as school boards, neighborhood policing, and urban planning, to name but a few.[37] PB stands in contrast with standard public budget making, where bureaucrats or elected politicians decide the allocation of public resources. There is also a more nuanced contrast with less empowered forms of deliberation that are not binding. These include deliberative polls, structured town halls, or large-scale participatory events, such as the ones AmericaSpeaks used to convene and conduct.[38]

Thus far, PB has been particularly effective in the United States at improving budgeting decisions when it has been implemented in local political ecosystems needing further transparency. The bulk of PB implementations have been with a portion of local municipal discretionary funds, often when elected officials had discretionary funds to use. This is a frequently neglected area that sometimes lacks transparency and accountability mechanisms. Across America, many local officials have discretionary funds. Perhaps these funds have received less attention than federal budget spending because they are distributed in smaller amounts and overall represent a small fraction of overall spending. Nonetheless, this is money that can directly benefit communities. PB efforts in the United States have shed light on some of these funds in a way that could bring about lasting institutional reform.

Participatory Budgeting in the United States

PB takes on a different flavor in each locality. Structural factors such as whether or not an NGO or a political party is instituting PB shape the process. The nature and format of the funding is a critical element. PB in the United States began in Chicago in 2009, when an alderman instituted a pilot project. Since then it has expanded across the country. In 2012 Vallejo, California, implemented the first citywide process. In 2014 Boston led the first youth-driven process for residents aged twelve to twenty-five years old called "Youth Lead the Change." New York City, meanwhile, has the largest implementation of PB in terms of allocated funds and related population. In New York twenty-four districts allocated roughly $32 million through PB in 2015.[39]

In the United States, PB has been championed by the **Participatory Budgeting Project** (PBP)[40], a nonprofit whose "mission is to empower people to decide together how to spend public money. [They] create and support participatory budgeting processes that deepen democracy, build stronger communities, and make public budgets more equitable and effective."[41] In each locality where it is active, PBP has worked closely with elected officials and CSOs to implement PB. PBP worked to adapt the process from Brazil for the municipal ward level in the United States providing education, technical assistance, and research and evaluation.[42] PBP worked to provide the support and expertise to enable PB to grow and flourish in the United States, including in New York City—which continues to be a critical site for PB in America.

Participatory Budgeting Comes to the Big Apple

In New York City, PBP worked closely with the membership-based Community Voices Heard (CVH), a nonprofit membership organization that organizes low-income populations located in one of the implementing districts. In 2010 PBP and CVH held two public events to garner support for PB.[43] CVH served as the community lead and PBP as the technical lead. PBP used its experience in bringing PB to the United States in Chicago to directly inform the structure of the process in New York City. CVH brought their networks and background organizing low-income populations. A large organizing effort helped bring PB to New York City, as Baez and Hernandez note: "The CMs [council members] had never heard of PB before being approached by community-based organizations."[44]

In 2011 four city council members, three Democrats and one Republican, decided that they would each put a portion of their discretionary funds into the hands of their constituents to let them decide how to allocate them. The process was decidedly bipartisan from its origins. The four council members each opted to put at least $1 million of their capital discretionary funds—used for physical infrastructure projects—into the process, with the option to add additional monies to fund other projects. They determined that each project selected must cost at least thirty-five thousand dollars and have a planned use of at least five years from the time of completion or installation. There were three main reasons the council members decided to restrict the project to capital funds: (1) There are stricter and clearer guidelines for capital funds; (2) Capital funds are less likely to be coopted by special interests or lobbying groups; and (3) Capital funds pertain to local infrastructure projects where local residents can offer expertise.

PB in New York City has seen a rapid expansion since the initial pilot in 2011. The leading partners on the steering committee offer stable roots: PBP is based out of New York City and CVH has strong community ties. These organizations have helped support the rise of the process. CVH Power (CVH's affiliated sister 501c4) did a considerable amount of work to expand the process and ensure that candidates for Speaker of the city council would be supportive of centralized infrastructure. For example, CVH Power sent out a questionnaire to all candidates for the council asking if they would implement PB if elected. The organization then posted the results on their website and got some news coverage about it as well. CVH and PBP held a briefing for council member candidates and then newly elected members. Thus, intentional organizing work went beyond the expansion of PB in New York City.

The organizing work paid off. One of the first implementing council members was subsequently elected Speaker of the city council. As PB efforts have grown across the country, at the time of this publication, New York City has maintained its prime position as the site of the largest experiment. PB in New York City continues to serve as an important petri dish for other cities in the United States that are looking to explore, adopt, and expand their own versions of PB.

New York City: An Emerging Hub for Civic Innovation

The politics of New York City is fascinating not only because it binds many interests together in intimate conflict but also because the stakes are so high. New York has long had the nation's largest, broadest, costliest, and most intrusive local public sector.[45] According to John Mollenkopf, the enormity of the public sector in New York City elevates the stakes of New York City politics. New York serves as an important petri dish for understanding PB in the United States.

Importantly, PB offers several opportunities for different types of engagement throughout the year, thus enabling people with different civic background and interests to participate in the process. Participatory Budgeting New York City (PBNYC) set up the following process calendar for the New York City pilot in 2011:[46]

- Planning
  A citywide steering committee designs the PB process. Project leads develop materials, raise supportive funding, and build relationships with local partners.
- Information Sessions
  Stakeholders in each district learn about the process of PB, what it is, and how they can get involved.
- Neighborhood Assemblies
  Stakeholders in each neighborhood learn about the available budget funds, brainstorm initial spending ideas, and volunteer to serve as budget delegates.

- Budget Delegate Meetings
Budget delegates meet in thematic issue committees (based on proposed ideas) to review project ideas, consult with government experts, fully develop project proposals, and prepare project posters and presentations.
- Second-Round Neighborhood Assemblies
Budget delegates present poster presentations in a science-fair format and neighborhood residents walk around, ask questions, and give project feedback. After this, budget delegates have time to incorporate feedback and prepare projects for the ballot.
- Voting (March)
Residents vote for which projects to fund in their districts.
- Evaluation, Implementation, and Monitoring
The council members work to implement the projects that receive the most votes. Ideally, citizens and civil society remain involved to evaluate the process and monitor project implementation.

The steering committee agreed upon the basic structure of the process whereby each district would have its own district committee, which would have local ownership over the various stages of the process, such as determining where to hold neighborhood assemblies and how to do outreach and mobilization.

PB, when compared to the status quo budgeting in New York, provides citizens more opportunities to flex their civic muscle and contribute to public decision making. The projects decided by PB have an additional degree of legitimacy—citizens are involved in every stage of the process. In traditional budget processes, citizens receive limited information about precisely where, why, or how a given project is decided upon and implemented.

I argue that PB transforms how those who participate understand themselves as citizens, constituents, council members, CSOs, and community stakeholders. It is not only the act of engaging in the process but the civic rewards and learning that result from the process as well. Unlike some traditional accounts of material rationales for civic involvement, I argue that participation in PB is maintained primarily because of transformative civic rewards. Despite considerable barriers to entry and obstacles to participation, citizens remained active participants in PBNYC pilot. Intangible civic rewards included greater civic knowledge, strengthened relationships with elected officials, greater community inclusion, and leadership combined with skill development.

PB is the result of a multistakeholder initiative tapping into existing strong civil society networks. During the initial pilot year of PBNYC, the first steps involved spreading the word about this new approach, led by PBP and CVH. This often included informal information sessions with an interactive component. Following on were neighborhood assemblies, where community residents identified where and how infrastructure funds could improve their area. At these assemblies, community stakeholders volunteered to serve as budget delegates, who were divided into thematic groups to reflect community priorities. Delegates and groups spent the next several months working closely with city agencies and meeting directly with government officials working on their issue set to craft viable budget proposals. After presenting and integrating more community feedback at a project expo, the projects were put to the wider community for a vote.

Each step requires resources from CSOs, council members, and citizens. Civil society leaders often volunteered their time to the process, working to galvanize traditionally marginalized people. Public officials also donated their time, often in the evening, to meet with budget delegate groups. Budget delegates often caravanned across the entire district to ensure that they listened to a diverse sampling of community needs, not simply the squeakiest wheel. An example includes a parks and recreation budget committee that surveyed every park in their district on a cold winter day a few days before Christmas.

Many people who participated, including many who had been active community participants for a long time, remarked on their satisfaction with the process. One even told me, "PBNYC is the most fulfilling mode of civic engagement I have ever been part of."[47] Primary reasons for this success may lie in the number of opportunities for knowledge transfer and direct contact with council members and city agencies—and in this way, PBNYC differs significantly from other forms of civic engagement, such as community boards, parent–teacher associations, and block associations.[48]

People want to feel connected and give back to their communities. PB provides hands-on civic education with government officials. Through participating in the process, people learn how government works. They also get to forge new relationships with others, and many people even learn something about themselves. They learn that civic engagement can be both rewarding and hard. At every scale, decision making requires navigating complexity and making difficult choices to effect political change. It's the unglamorous, hard, sustained work of governance that can create better democratic conditions and bring about stronger communities.

There are many different theories about why people choose to be active in their communities. Some scholars posit that people engage in PB in particular due to its perceived effectiveness.[49] In contrast, I argue that many citizens found satisfaction in this form of sustained participation not necessarily because of its effectiveness in terms such as material service delivery improvement or putting forth a specific proposal but rather because of PB's civic rewards.[50] In my interviews, participants routinely cite the number of opportunities for knowledge transfer, leadership development, and direct contact with government officials and agencies as the primary reasons the process is a uniquely engaging civic activity.

Implementing PB in the New York City council suggests that democratic experiments can flourish even within political ecosystems that perhaps seem unlikely for reform.[51] PB continues to expand in New York City. In her "State of the City" address in early 2015, New York City Council Speaker Melissa Mark-Viverito called for PB to be applied to parts of the Tenant Participation Activity funds within New York City Housing Authority funds for public housing.[52] The very presence of, and continued expansion of, PB of New York City and across the country suggests that there may be some political leeway to experiment and innovate. These processes require robust civic society support, political buy-in, and managing political motivations. To date in the United States, only a portion of municipal budgets have been put toward the process.

Expanding PB across the United States

The Obama White House pledged to support PB as part of international **Open Government Partnership**[53] commitments. The Second Open Government National Action Plan includes a PB commitment: "In 2014, the Administration will work in collaboration with the Strong Cities, Strong Communities initiative (SC2), the National League of Cities, non-profit organizations, philanthropies, and interested cities to: create tools and best practices that communities can use to implement projects; raise awareness among other American communities that PB can be used to help determine local investment priorities; and help educate communities on PB and its benefits."[54] In 2011 the United States helped launch the Open Government Partnership with eight member countries (Brazil, Indonesia, Mexico, Norway, the Philippines, South Africa, the United Kingdom, and the United

States); to date it includes sixty-six member nations.[55] The countries in this international multistakeholder partnership pledge themselves to greater citizen participation and advancing government transparency and accountability. Importantly, the Open Government Partnership also establishes a direct dialogue between CSOs and governments—empowering CSOs as coproducers. Each participating nation puts forth an "action plan" listing their open government pledges toward enacting these core principles.

As the open government and innovation policy advisor in the White House Office of Science and Technology Policy, I worked on the Obama administration's second term open government agenda—including work toward the second national action plan. Some localities across the country are beginning to experiment with ways to incorporate a PB process within community development block grants from the U.S. Department of Housing and Urban Development.[56]

In general, I do not view PB as divorced from other innovations to revitalize civic, communal, and democratic life.[57] I argue that PB is best understood as part of a vibrant civic infrastructure to reimagine how to implement democracy in the networked era. The inclusion of PB in the national action plan illustrates the interplay between federal support and bottom-up driven initiatives. Ultimately, I view the engagements occurring on the local level as collective efforts to empower citizens in their localities. The federal government and other entities such as foundations can at times provide support and exposure to illustrate best practices and connect like-minded innovators. Because these innovations occur in and out of civil society, the emphasis cannot be solely on government actors. Rather, innovations ought to leverage a multisector approach including the private sector, civil society, and academia.

Engaging Citizens: Beyond Participatory Budgeting

Empowering citizens in their communities will take a multifaceted approach offering several types of engagement. The PB process itself offers several different levels of engagement—from coming out to vote once to being involved over several months to craft viable rules. Some citizens may be interested to volunteer to mobilize their neighbors. Others may be more interested to directly engage with policymakers and learn about the process of governance. I provide two brief illustrative examples, in addition to PB, of ways for citizens to engage in policymaking.

Example 1: Technology Empowering People to Inform Public Policy

What happens after an election? Typically when citizens come out to vote, that is the end of their direct involvement in shaping public policy. One critical function of public policy is setting the agenda for a new administration. Yet there is a disconnect between an administration setting new priorities and the opportunities for individuals to effectively express their distinct preferences apart from voting itself. While there are community groups with strong ties to elected officials, many everyday residents are not engaged.

Talking Transition NYC[58], funded by philanthropies including the Open Society Foundation, was an experiment to engage New Yorkers to express their preferences to inform a new mayoral transition to Mayor de Blasio. The goal was to create a new digital and in-person interactive experience to foster civic engagement and public dialogue. Nearly seventy thousand people shared their view on city services. There was also a robust social media presence where people could give feedback in real time through Twitter, Facebook, and Instagram.

In addition to digital tools, Talking Transition NYC featured a physical convening tent, which nearly fifteen thousand people visited over the course of more than two weeks immediately following Election Day. The tent housed touch pads and online kiosks where people could write down priorities for the next mayor and give their feedback. Social media was displayed throughout the tent—providing a further platform for people's individual preferences to be listened to.

Talking Transition NYC created one of the most expansive public-opinion surveys in New York history. Supplementing online tools were in-person canvassers who spoke nineteen languages. The finished report outlined eleven key initiatives of pressing concern to New Yorkers. More research is needed to understand how these views are translated into improved policy outcomes, but the model serves as an illustrative lesson on creative ways to structure civic feedback and frame political transitions.[59]

Example 2: Technology Empowering People to Fund Public Works

Communities throughout the United States have faced budget constraints since the recession. Local governments face an increased demand to provide services with shrinking budgets. Central Falls, Rhode Island, a dense city of twenty thousand people, declared chapter 9 bankruptcy in August 2011. As a result, many city projects lack resources or staff capacity.

Seeking to address such conditions, the city partnered with a civic crowd-funding platform, **Citizinvestor**[60], to offer cutting-edge public funding and engagement models. Much like Kickstarter, the platform enables individuals to pledge dollar amounts. Individual investors are not charged unless the project reaches the full funding goal. Residents identified new trash cans as a neighborhood priority. Lacking in proper trash bins and recycling, the local park was littered with trash from overflowing bins.

Sixty-eight people donated the money to purchase new trash cans. The city partnered with a local nonprofit to design new trash/recycling containers for the park. The new trash bins are a work of art that brought out diverse community members both young and old to contribute to the installation. People were involved throughout the process—from determining priorities to providing input and dollars.

Central Falls' use of Citizinvestor provides an important model for others to follow and demonstrates that online platforms can harness the power of individual, often small donations toward creating public goods. More research is needed to understand precisely at what scale and how to create proper safeguards. However, in times of increased fiscal scarcity, this may offer an avenue for civic engagement.

Next Steps

Cities are gaining momentum as incubators for innovation. States and cities are in fact the "laboratories of democracy." The locality is reemerging as a sphere for inclusive governance.[61] In a world of ubiquitous communication, density is sometimes a stronger indicator than geography. Cities can learn best practices from one another. Sharing this information can build a strong foundation to amplify and encourage experimentation.

Inclusive governance is not bound only to urban areas. More broadly than cities, the local level, including rural and exurbs, provides a more manageable size for citizens to be more closely connected to the policies that impact them the most. There could be a large value add to harness and connect local initiatives to national or international policy. This in turn could help ensure that individual initiatives can be meshed together to improve governance.

Increasingly, multistakeholder models leveraging public and private partnerships are catalyzing innovation. Examples involve public–private partnerships incorporating resources from the private sector, universities, and the entire civil/social sector, broadly defined.

Governments should not necessarily build new platforms but rather should create channels to support citizens and their already existing networks. Networks are digital, hyperlocal, and global. Experimentation is necessary to test and pioneer diverse strategies in localities of different sizes.

A strategy can engage local officials from municipal leaders to mayors as well as federal officials working in parallel. Civil society can engage public officials as genuine partners and create mutually agreed-upon timelines and deliverables—with opportunities to revise them. Civil society can also work to support the state and local efforts toward inclusive governance. For example, the post-2015 sustainable development goals feature Goal 16.7, which calls on signatories to "ensure responsive, inclusive, participatory and representative decision-making at all levels."[62]

Many governments fear that engaging citizens will lead to further vulnerability—heightened criticism and an influx of demands for reduced resources. How can inclusive governance enable and build support for choices rather than the presentation of demands? Civil society can construct coalitions to build up resources, including partnerships with the private sector. Additionally, civil society can work to reduce the perceived political costs of inclusive governance by, for example, publicly acknowledging the limits inherent to government and working to buttress, not only critique, them. Creating metrics and indicators of success that reflect process outputs, not only outcomes, can address this. For example, a metric of inclusive governance can include the ways in which elected officials are genuinely engaged with the public, the availability of accurate information, and the creation of timely accountability channels. Metrics can underscore that sometimes outputs are important outcomes that can lay the foundation for deeper civic participation. Civil society can help foster the conditions for more successful innovation, experimentation, and sustainability—if properly executed.

In the United States there is a beginning wave of commitments from elected officials about more inclusive governance concentrated on the local level. There are numerous questions about its authenticity, accountability, and potential obsolescence. Are these elected officials primarily interested in electoral gain? Are these processes uniquely ripe for co-option and corruption? Can civil society ensure legitimacy, continuity between government transitions, and sustained participation? Furthermore, can civil society work in tandem with governance institutions in a bridging capacity? Government—at all levels—needs to commit to this vision of a more robust role of everyday citizens in policymaking and leverage digital tools to so do. A goal is a deepened civic infrastructure for political engagement.

Civil society can identify and foster conditions under which inclusive governance is more or less likely to grow. As a result, strategic choices can build up communal resilience. For example, Mount Rainer, Maryland, has a strong civic community that engages citizens. Their tool library and bike share engage a large swath of this perhaps self-selecting community.[63] Anchor institutions are one ingredient of success: the Community Forklift home improvement center and Joe's Movement Emporium performing arts center offer education on production and artist services.[64] Anchor institutions help foster face-to-face engagement and networks of trust that are more important than ever in a highly digital world. Yet some organizations have fewer resources for process support, which can include capacity to mobilize people and keep them involved. A strategy could find and strengthen existing anchor institutions across localities and could provide support and resources. Citizens need to take responsibility for their communities. Instead of further disillusionment with politics, digital tools can foster new entry points for civic engagement.

Civil society can play a role as a reliable civic intermediary to provide citizens with a "civic layer" for their lives. Citizens currently lack trust in governing institutions and basic heuristics to understand *how and where to participate*. Every day, citizens are inundated with too much information. At the same time, most citizens lack basic information about their public systems or opportunities for engagement. This can take many forms—for example, a centralized public sphere such as Boston's District Hall, a community center, post office, or a library. This could also include a centralized online repository, with integrated offline components, of how citizens can engage—who, what, where, when, and why. Offline components can capitalize on already vibrant civic community centers.

Online tools can buttress, support, and enhance existing opportunities. Building broad and deep inclusive governance that is resilient to elections will require online tools. However, digital tools simply cannot replace the face-to-face interaction that is more important than ever.

Working toward inclusive governance takes more nuanced indicators and metrics. Building the capacity and opportunity for inclusive governance will require understanding politics and institutions. Technology alone cannot change this reality. Participation is more than the numbers of "clicks," "total page views," or "contacts." It is also about their *nature* and quality, including genuine opportunities for deliberation and dialogue.

Conclusion

Can these innovations help return politics to the locality? Maybe. They attempt to rescue politics from elitism. Gary Zajac and John G. Bruhn argue that the Weberian hierarchical-bureaucratic model has been unable to foster inclusive and robust relationships between citizens and their elected officials.[65] I argue that civic innovation can enable new channels for deepening democracy. The examples provided, and PB in particular, offer a reimagined public sphere where citizens can engage. Through these new mechanisms, citizens can be the architects of their participation and craft new models for a more participatory democracy. In the digital era, the power of face to face interaction with neighbors, elected officials, and community members is more important than ever, not less. Improved democratic conditions may yield a renewed civic spirit in a community, stronger relationships with neighbors, or renewed faith in governance.

The goal is civic knowledge and empowerment. Government has never been simply about the most efficient service delivery. The public sphere, or polis, was always about something greater than our individual selves.

Aristotle famously defined man as uniquely capable of speech. Aristotle's *"zoon logon echon"* is understood as a "living being capable of speech."[66] It is this capacity that sets man apart from other animals. Hannah Arendt, who saw herself as advancing on Aristotle's major themes, further explains: "The organized polis is the highest form of human communal life and thus something specifically human, at equal remove from the gods, who can exist in and of themselves in full freedom and independence, and animals, whose communal life, if they have such a thing, is a matter of necessity."[67] To engage in politics is to engage in a type of freedom unique to mankind.

These processes may not be a democratic panacea, but they do open up spaces for civic creativity. If successfully implemented, the rewards outweigh the costs. Civic innovations can create small instances wherein citizens can escape from confined roles and engage with neighbors, communities, and governance in a transformed capacity. This can even include opportunities for knowledge sharing, leadership development, and new friendships. When citizens participate in more inclusive governance, they are suddenly engaging with their neighbors and elected officials in *nontraditional* roles. This takes place in physical as well as digital spaces and networks. Perhaps if we keep trying and showing willingness for experimentation, the result could be stronger civic, communal, and democratic life in America. Maybe the public sphere can be ignited for the twenty-first century.

Notes

Preface

1. John Dewey, *Democracy and Education* (New York: Free Press, 1997), available online at: https://www.gutenberg.org/files/852/852-h/852-h.htm.

2. Hollie Russon Gilman, *Democracy Reinvented: Participatory Budgeting and Civic Innovation in America* (Washington, DC: Brookings Institution Press with the Ash Center for Democratic Governance and Innovation, Harvard University, Kennedy School of Government, 2016).

3. Community Development Project at the Urban Justice Center and the Participatory Budgeting in New York City Research Team, *A People's Budget: A Research and Evaluation Report on Participatory Budgeting in New York City* (New York: Urban Justice Center, 2012). Available online at https://cdp.urbanjustice.org/sites/default/files/pbreport.pdf.

Participatory Budgeting and Civic Tech

1. Throughout this work, the term "citizen" denotes someone with the political standing to exercise voice or give consent over public decisions, not legal citizenship.

2. National Conference on Citizenship, the Center for Information and Research on Civic Learning and Engagement, Mobilize.org, and the Institute of Politics, Harvard University, *Millennials Civic Health Index* (Washington, DC: National Conference on Citizenship, 2013).

3. See Nathaniel Heller, "The Sharing Economy Is Not Civic Tech," *Global Integrity*, www.globalintegrity.org/2013/12/the-sharing-economy-is-not-civic-tech/.

4. See Laurenellen McCann, *Experimental Modes of Civic Engagement in Civic Tech* (Chicago: Smart Chicago Collaborative, 2015).

5. See Stephen Goldsmith and Susan Crawford, *The Responsive City: Engaging Communities through Data-Smart Governance* (San Francisco: Jossey-Bass, 2014); and B. S. Noveck, *Smart Citizens, Smarter State: The Technologies of Expertise and the Future of Governing* (Cambridge, MA: Harvard University Press, 2015).

6. Mark E. Warren, "What Should We Expect from More Democracy? Radically Democratic Responses to Politics." *Political Theory* 24, no. 2 (May 1996): 241–70. doi:10.1177/0090591796024002004.

7. Soni Sangha, "Putting in Their 2 Cents," *New York Times,* March 30, 2012, http://www.nytimes.com/2012/04/01/nyregion/for-some-new-yorkers-a-grand-experiment-in-participatory-budgeting.html; see also Soni Sangha, "The Voters Speak: Yes to Bathrooms," *New York Times,* April 6, 2012, http://www.nytimes.com/2012/04/08/nyregion/voters-speak-in-budget-experiment-saying-yes-to-bathrooms.html.

8. New York City Council, "Participatory Budgeting," 2015, http://council.nyc.gov/html/pb/home.shtml.

9. Josh Lerner, *Everyone Counts: Could "Participatory Budgeting" Change Democracy?* (Ithaca, NY: Cornell Selects, Cornell University Press, 2014).

10. For PB experiments in a Phoenix high school, see Zocalo Public Square, "How Would Students Spend the Principal's Money," *Time,* March 11, 2015, http://time.com/3740510/phoenix-budgeting-experiment/.

11. Office of the Mayor (Seattle, Mayor Edward B. Murray), "Mayor, Licata Announce Participatory Budgeting Project," July 7, 2015, http://murray.seattle.gov/mayor-licata-announce-participatory-budgeting-project/#sthash.CGrMUbBc.dpbs.

12. Nick Sinai and Gayle Smith, "The United States Releases Its Second Open Government National Action Plan," *White House* (blog), December 6, 2013, https://www.whitehouse.gov/blog/2013/12/06/united-states-releases-its-second-open-government-national-action-plan.

13. See Clean Air Coalition of Western New York, "Implement Participatory Budgeting in Buffalo!" online petition, 2015, http://www.change.org/p/mayor-byron-brown-implement-participatory-budgeting-in-buffalo?source_location=update_footer&algorithm=promoted.

14. Plato, *Laws* 5.738a.

15. Yves Sintomer, Carsten Herzberg, and Giovanni Allegretti, with Anja Röcke, "Learning from the South: Participatory Budgeting Worldwide—an Invitation to Global Cooperation," *Dialog Global,* no. 25 (December 2010), http://www.service-eine-welt.de/images/text_material-2152.img.

16. Richelle Harrison Plesse, "Parisians Have Their Say on City's First €20m 'Participatory Budget,'" *Guardian,* October 8, 2014, http://www.theguardian.com/cities/2014/oct/08/parisians-have-say-city-first-20m-participatory-budget.

17. Anwar Shah, ed. *Participatory Budgeting* (Washington, DC: World Bank, 2007); and Felip Estefan and Boris Weber, "Mobile-Enhanced Participatory Budgeting in the DRC," *Information and Communications for Development* (blog), February 13, 2012, http://blogs.worldbank.org/ic4d/mobile-enhanced -participatory-budgeting-in-the-drc.

18. Brian Wampler, "Expanding Accountability through Participatory Institutions: Mayors, Citizens, and Budgeting in Three Brazilian Municipalities," *Latin American Politics and Society* 46, no. 2 (2004): 73–99; and Benjamin Goldfrank, "Lessons from Latin America's Experience in Participatory Budgeting," in *Participatory Budgeting*, ed. Anwar Shah, 91–121 (Washington, DC: World Bank, 2007).

19. See Brian Wampler and Leonardo Avritzer, "Participatory Publics: Civil Society and New Institutions in Democratic Brazil," *Comparative Politics* 36, no. 3 (April 2004): 291–312, doi:10.2307/4150132; and Brian Wampler, "Can Participatory Institutions Promote Pluralism? Mobilizing Low-Income Citizens in Brazil," *Studies in Comparative International Development (SCID)* 41, no. 4 (December 2007): 57–78, doi:10.1007/BF02800471.

20. Brian Wampler, "A Guide to Participatory Budgeting," in *Participatory Budgeting*, ed. Anwar Shah, 21–54 (Washington, DC: World Bank, 2007), 20.

21. Wampler, "Can Participatory Institutions Promote Pluralism?"

22. Brian Wampler, *Participatory Budgeting in Brazil: Contestation, Cooperation, and Accountability* (University Park: Pennsylvania State University Press, 2007).

23. For greater discussion, see Wampler, "Can Participatory Institutions Promote Pluralism?"

24. Michael Touchton and Brian Wampler, "Improving Social Well-Being through New Democratic Institutions." *Comparative Political Studies* 47, no. 10 (2014): 1442–69, doi:10.1177/0010414013512601.

25. Ibid., 1444.

26. Sónia Gonçalves, 2014. "The Effect of Participatory Budgeting on Municipal Expenditures and Infant Mortality in Brazil." *World Development* 53 (2014): 94–110, doi:10.1016/j.worlddev.2013.01.009.

27. Paolo Spada, "The Economic and Political Effects of Participatory Budgeting" (paper presented at the Annual Conference of the Latin American Studies Association, Rio de Janeiro, June 11–14, 2009).

28. Benjamin Goldfrank, "Urban Experiments in Citizen Participation: Deepening Democracy in Latin America" (PhD diss., University of California at Berkeley, 2002).

29. Goldfrank, "Lessons from Latin America's Experience," 95.

30. Shah, *Participatory Budgeting*, 1.

31. Wampler, "A Guide to Participatory Budgeting," 22.

32. Boaventura de Sousa Santos, "Participatory Budgeting in Porto Alegre: Toward a Redistributive Democracy," in *Democratizing Democracy: Beyond the*

Liberal Democratic Canon, ed. Boaventura de Sousa Santos, 307–76 (New York: Verso, 2005), available at http://www.boaventuradesousasantos.pt/media/Chapter %2011.pdf.

33. Malina Novkirishka-Stoyanova, "Legislative Framework Supporting Citizen Participation in Local Government in Bulgaria" (paper presented at the Local Government Initiative, Research Triangle Institute, Sofia, Bulgaria, 2001).

34. On increased forms of participation for legitimacy, see Donald P. Moynihan, "Normative and Instrumental Perspectives on Public Participation: Citizen Summits in Washington, DC," *American Review of Public Administration* 33, no. 2 (2003): 164–88; and Christiane Olivo, "The Practical Problems of Bridging Civil Society and the State: A Study of Round Tables in Eastern Germany," *Polity* 31, no. 2 (1998): 244–68, doi:10.2307/3235228. On a trend toward transparency, see Donald P. Moynihan, "Citizen Participation in Budgeting: Prospects for Developing Countries," in *Participatory Budgeting*, ed. Anwar Shah, 55–83 (Washington, DC: World Bank 2007). On a trend toward fiscal decentralization, see M. Robinson, "Resources, Citizen Engagement, and Democratic Local Governance" (paper for a project-planning workshop organized by Resources, Citizen Engagement, and Democratic Local Governance [ReCitE], Thiruvananthapuram, Kerala, India, January 4–16, 2004).

35. Judith Edstrom, "Indonesia's Kecamatan Development Project: Is It Replicable? Design Considerations in Community Driven Development," *Social Development Papers*, no. 39 (March 2002), available at www-wds.worldbank.org /servlet/WDSContentServer/WDSP/IB/2005/02/22/000009486_20050222171656 /Rendered/PDF/316150SDP13901public1.pdf.

36. Rosemary McGee, with Nyangabyaki Bazaara, Jonathan Gaventa, Rose Nierras, Manoj Rai, Joel Rocamora, Nelson Saule Jr., Emma Williams, and Sergio Zermeño, "Legal Frameworks for Citizen Participation: Synthesis Report," LogoLink, April 2003.

37. On neighborhood policing, see Archon Fung, *Empowered Participation: Reinventing Urban Democracy* (Princeton, NJ: Princeton University Press, 2004). On urban planning, see Jeffery M. Berry, Kent E. Portney, Robin Liss, Jessica Simoncelli, and Lisa Berger, "Power and Interest Groups in City Politics," Rappaport Institute for Greater Boston, December 2006), available at http://citeseerx .ist.psu.edu/viewdoc/download?doi=10.1.1.133.7133&rep=rep1&type=pdf.

38. See James S. Fishkin, *Democracy and Deliberation: New Directions for Democratic Reform* (New Haven, CT: Yale University Press, 1993). AmericaSpeaks was a nonprofit organization (1995–2014) that organized large-scale deliberative dialogues to engage citizens on key policy issues. See AmericaSpeaks, "AmericaSpeaks: A Legacy of Critical Innovations in Deliberative Democracy and Citizen Engagement" (online pamphlet, 2014), https://dl.dropboxusercontent.com/u/6405436 /AmericaSpeaks_Legacy.pdf.

39. New York City Council, "Participatory Budgeting," 2015 http://council .nyc.gov/html/pb/home.shtml.

40. http://www.participatorybudgeting.org/.

41. Participatory Budgeting Project, "Mission & Approach," 2014, http://www .participatorybudgeting.org/who-we-are/mission-approach/.

42. Josh Lerner and Donata Secondo, "By the People, for the People: Participatory Budgeting from the Bottom up in North America," *Journal of Public Deliberation* 8, no. 2 (2012): art. 2, http://www.publicdeliberation.net/jpd/vol8/iss2 /art2; and Lerner, *Everyone Counts*.

43. See Lerner, *Everyone Counts*; and Nancy Baez and Andreas Hernandez, "Participatory Budgeting in the City: Challenging NYC's Development Paradigm from the Grassroots," *Interface: A Journal for and about Social Movements* 4, no. 1 (2012): 316–26, esp. 319–23, the section titled "The Long Road from the World Social Forums to NYC."

44. Baez and Hernandez, "Participatory Budgeting in the City," 324.

45. John H. Mollenkopf, *A Phoenix in the Ashes: The Rise and Fall of the Koch Coalition in New York City Politics* (Princeton, NJ: Princeton University Press, 1992), 13.

46. Community Development Project at the Urban Justice Center and the Participatory Budgeting in New York City Research Team, *A People's Budget*.

47. This statement was offered by one long-standing community board member.

48. New York City has fifty-nine community boards that serve as appointed advisors on a range of city matters including land use zoning, community concerns, and the city's budget. Unlike in PB, community board members serve only in an advisory capacity.

49. Leonardo Avritzer, "Modes of Democratic Deliberation: Participatory Budgeting in Brazil," in *Democratizing Democracy: Beyond the Liberal Democratic Canon*, ed. Boaventura de Sousa Santos, 377–404 (London: Verso, 2006).

50. Again, I use the term "citizen" to refer to people engaged in civic processes, including especially participants in PB. I am not referring to formal citizenship status.

51. New York City Council, "Participatory Budgeting," http://council.nyc.gov /html/pb/home.shtml.

52. Council of the City of New York, Office of Communications, "Speaker Melissa Mark-Viverito Delivers 2015 State of the City Address," press release, February 11, 2015, http://council.nyc.gov/html/pr/021115soc.shtml; and Sondra Youdelman, "NYC Speaker Melissa Mark-Viverito Announces New Resources and New Decision-Making Power for NYC Housing Authority Residents," Community Voices Heard (Website), February 14, 2015, http://www.cvhaction.org /node/654.

53 http://www.opengovpartnership.org/.

54. "The Open Government Partnership: Second Open Government National Action Plan for the United States of America," December 5, 2013, p. 10, http://www.whitehouse.gov/sites/default/files/docs/us_national_action_plan_6p.pdf.

55. Current membership as of 2014. For more information, see their website, OpenGovPartnership.org.

56. https://www.hudexchange.info/manage-a-program/participatory-budgeting/.

57. I have collaborated closely with Georgia Bullen and Laurenellen McCann on writings on civic innovation, including on frameworks, metrics, and typologies. For an extended take on this topic, see writings at New America's Open Technology Institute.

58. http://www.talkingtransition2013.com/.

59. For more on technology, see also Hollie Russon Gilman, "More Inclusive Governance in the Digital Age" Data-Smart City Solutions, June 17, 2015, http://datasmart.ash.harvard.edu/news/article/more-inclusive-governance-in-the-digital-age-699.

60. http://www.citizinvestor.com/project/clean-up-cf-new-bins-in-jenks-park.

61. People have always been coming together in their communities; however, these efforts are now receiving a broader international spotlight coupled with the emergence of digital tools.

62. See United Nations, Sustainable Development Knowledge Platform, "Open Working Group Proposal for Sustainable Development Goals," https://sustainabledevelopment.un.org/sdgsproposal.

63. Mount Rainer Bike Coop Website, http://mrbikecoop.blogspot.com/; and Mount Rainer Community Toolshed Website, www.communitytoolshed.org.

64. Community Forklift Website, CommunityForklift.org; and Joe's Movement Emporium Website, JoesMovement.org.

65. Gary Zajac and John G. Bruhn, "The Moral Context of Participation in Planned Organizational Change and Learning," *Administration and Society* 30, no. 6 (1999): 706–33, doi:10.1177/00953999922019058.

66. Hannah Arendt, *The Human Condition*, 2nd ed. (Chicago: University of Chicago Press, 1998).

67. Hannah Arendt, *The Promise of Politics* (New York: Schocken, 2005), 116.

Acknowledgments

The author thanks Daniel Benaim, Georgia Bullen, Phil Caruso, Archon Fung, Claudine Gay, Elizabeth Guernsey, Brooke Hunter, Adam Lebowitz, Josh Lerner, Laurenellen McCann, Quinton Mayne, Nathan McKee, Beth Noveck, Sabeel K. Rahman, Andrea Batista Schlesinger, Donata Secondo, Paolo Spada, Dennis Thompson, Sondra Youdelman, and the Open Society Foundations.

About the Author

Hollie Russon Gilman previously served as policy adviser on open government and innovation in the White House Office of Science and Technology Policy. She is a postdoctoral research scholar at Columbia University's School of International and Public Affairs, a fellow at New America, an adviser for Data for Social Good at Georgetown University's McCourt School of Public Policy, and Visiting Fellow at Georgetown's Beeck Center for Social Impact and Innovation. She holds a PhD in government from Harvard University's Kennedy School of Government and is the author of *Democracy Reinvented: Participatory Budgeting and Civic Innovation in America* (Ash Institute for Democratic Governance and Innovation, 2016).

CPSIA information can be obtained
at www.ICGtesting.com
Printed in the USA
BVHW022043201118
533679BV00033B/737/P

9 781626 163409